THE TELEPHONE SKILLS POCKETBOOK

2nd Edition

By Mary Richards

Drawings by Phil Hailstone

"Excellent! Master these essential techniques, take control of all your phone calls and get more out of each day."
Mike Richards, Sales and Marketing Director, Liquid Drop Ltd

"A powerful message for anyone who needs to project a professional and dynamic image over the telephone. I certainly want to be a super-user."
Samantha Reynolds, Helpdesk Supervisor, Canon Helpdesk, Canon (UK) Ltd

CONTENTS

INTRODUCTION

THE TELEPHONE

In 1876 Alexander Graham Bell demonstrated and patented the telephone.

Well over 100 years later the telephone is still evolving and continues to revolutionise the way we communicate.

'Tele' from the Greek 'afar, far off'; 'phone' from the Greek 'sound, voice'.

CORE BUSINESS COMPONENTS

While developing technologies provide continuous advancements in communication systems and methods, the telephone remains a core component of business communications.

CORE OR COMMONPLACE?

As the telephone has moved from being a rare commodity to a commonplace item, our relationship with it has changed. We take it for granted.

We forget that it is both:

- A business tool and
- A communications vehicle

As such, the telephone should be viewed as a key business asset.

> 'An amazing invention – but who would ever want to use one?'

Rutherford B. Hayes
American statesman and President 1822-1893

A BUSINESS ASSET

The telephone is a real asset when:

- ✔ Taking orders from customers
- ✔ Improving customer service
- ✔ Providing a help line
- ✔ Communicating with colleagues
- ✔ Working remotely
- ✔ Making life easier
- ✔ Saving time
- ✔ Saving money

However...

A BUSINESS LIABILITY

...the telephone is a true liability when:

- ✗ It isn't answered
- ✗ The telephone manner is inappropriate
- ✗ Information, facts and figures are 'misheard'
- ✗ Calls are not responded to
- ✗ The service provided is questionable
- ✗ Over-automation exasperates the caller

WHAT MAKES THE DIFFERENCE?

The only difference between the telephone being an ASSET or a LIABILITY is...

YOU

INTRODUCTION

YOUR RELATIONSHIP WITH THE TELEPHONE

You love the telephone when it:

- Saves you time
- Makes your job easier
- Keeps you in touch
- Helps you stay in control
- Makes you feel popular
- Keeps you up to date
- Gives you instant access to people
  and information
- Helps you to get things done
- Acts as a life-line

In fact, there are times when you feel you
couldn't live without each other.

YOUR RELATIONSHIP WITH THE TELEPHONE

You loathe the telephone when it:

- Demands your attention
- Disrupts your train of thought
- Forces you to reorganise your plans
- Makes you late
- Increases the pressure
- Invades your space
- Wastes your time
- Doesn't give you a moment's peace

ARE YOU ALWAYS A SUPER-USER?

Attitudes, telephone manners and techniques differ widely. Maybe you're a Super-User:

Attitude - The phone is a useful tool that must earn its keep

Manner - Courteous and efficient

Technique - You know what you want to achieve

- You know what you want to say

- You get straight to the point and keep to it

- You know when to say goodbye

OR SOMETIMES A CASUAL-USER?

Attitude - 'The phone is a commonplace item – who needs skills to use it?'

Manner - Casual to the point of being careless

Technique - You don't have one!

Note On the scale of Super to Casual, you'll probably hover at different points depending on the situation, your mood or the pressure you're under. Maybe you're 'super' at handling customer complaints, but come down a few notches if you need to make a sales call. Or perhaps you're less 'casual' when your job depends on the call or when the boss comes by!

CONSIDER YOUR TELEPHONE SKILLS

Have you ever:

- Continued doing other things while on the telephone ?
- Said you'd call back - and then didn't ?
- Let the phone ring unanswered ?
- Had to make a second call because you forgot to ask about...?
- Pretended you've been cut off ?
- Made faces to your colleagues about the person on the other end of the phone ?
- Lost callers while transferring them to another extension ?
- Claimed to be someone else ("Sorry, everyone seems to have gone home - I'm only the cleaner") ?
- Asked the caller to hold while you fetch a pen and paper ?
- Been caught out because you 'didn't confirm it in writing' ?
- Lifted a ringing receiver and replaced it at once ?
- Had to ask callers to repeat themselves because you were distracted ?

CONSIDER YOUR TELEPHONE SKILLS

Or, maybe you've said:

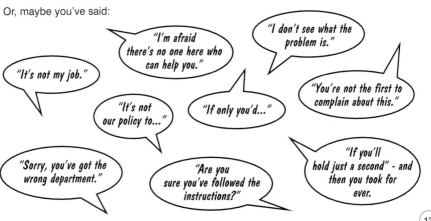

"I'm afraid there's no one here who can help you."

"I don't see what the problem is."

"It's not my job."

"You're not the first to complain about this."

"It's not our policy to..."

"If only you'd..."

"Sorry, you've got the wrong department."

"Are you sure you've followed the instructions?"

"If you'll hold just a second" - and then you took for ever.

SUPER-USER V CASUAL-USER

So, Super-User or Casual-User, which is it to be?

After all, what have you got to lose:

- Customers?
- Orders?
- Opportunities?
- Business?
- Credibility?
- Promotion?
- Your job?

The big question is, 'Can you afford not to be a **SUPER-USER**?'

YOU AS A COMMUNICATOR

WHEN COMMUNICATION FAILS

- Mistakes are made
- Misunderstandings occur
- Time is wasted
- Problems are created
- Relationships are strained
- Orders are lost
- Information is incorrect
- Instructions become misleading
- Reality is distorted
- Confusion arises
- Opportunities are missed
- People complain
- Customers change suppliers

SOUNDS FAMILIAR?

When you're on the phone have you ever:

- Been asked to repeat something you've said?
- Taken a sip of coffee or continued 'snacking'?
- Had to ask for information to be repeated because you weren't listening?
- Failed to record what was agreed?
- Tried to make a sales call when you weren't feeling at your best?
- Misunderstood someone?
- Started to speak at the same time as the other person?
- Purposefully responded in a leisurely and laid-back way to a caller who was obviously in a great hurry?
- Taken down information incorrectly - maybe an incorrect phone number?

THE PRINCIPLES

COMMUNICATION IS MORE THAN WORDS

"I'm starting a new job tomorrow."
Is the speaker enthusiastic or
nervous, delighted
or reluctant?

To answer the question you
need to be able to:

- **Hear** the tone of voice,
  the intonation, the volume

- **See** the facial expressions,
  the gestures, the body
  language

YOU AS A COMMUNICATOR

THE PRINCIPLES

COMMUNICATION IS ABOUT WHAT WE SEE AND HEAR

Communication is about:

WORDS

PARALINGUISTICS – the way they're said

BODY LANGUAGE – the actions that accompany them

All three elements contribute to the overall meaning.

Studies show that, when we need clarification, we place more emphasis on what we see than on what we hear. So when you're communicating on the phone you need to compensate for what cannot be seen.

YOU AS A COMMUNICATOR

THE PRINCIPLES
YOUR WORDS

- Choose your words carefully because the listener hasn't got the benefit of being able to see you
- Use words that will put the listener in the picture
- Avoid ambiguous words
- During the conversation, check from time to time that the listener understands your meaning
- Spell difficult or confusing words – 'Joe Easton' can sound like ' Jo Eastem'
- Repeat and check names, phone numbers, instructions and directions – '6 to 8' can easily be mistaken for '68' or '628'

YOU AS A COMMUNICATOR

THE PRINCIPLES

YOUR VOICE

- Speak clearly
- Speak directly into the mouthpiece
- Your posture affects your voice - don't slump in the chair
- If you need to sound more assertive, stand up
- Use emphasis in your voice to reinforce your words
- Be efficient but friendly - efficiency without friendliness can make you sound brusque
- If you cannot hear your caller's voice clearly, tell him/her

THE PRINCIPLES

YOUR BODY LANGUAGE

- Use body language even though it can't be seen - without it you will sound wooden, stilted, lifeless
- Smile - even though it will not be seen, it will be 'heard'
- Focus your eyes in the mid distance or on something that will help you to concentrate on your communication
- Learn to listen for body language - listen to pauses and breathing patterns

THE PRINCIPLES

BARRIERS TO COMMUNICATION

The biggest single barrier to effective communication on the phone is that with most equipment we can't see each other. However, there are other barriers:

- Noise - on the line, in the background or around you
- Distractions - you try to do something else, or someone attracts your attention while you're on the phone
- Language - the use of jargon, acronyms, poor enunciation or an unfamiliar accent can lead to misunderstandings

As a Super-User you can reduce the barriers by:

- Keeping the noise around you to a minimum
- Turning your back on any activity or distraction
- Focusing solely on the phone call
- Speaking plainly and clearly
- Checking for understanding

THE PRACTICE

CALL WHEN YOU'RE AT YOUR BEST

- Whenever possible, make calls when you feel and look your best; some people are more alert in the morning, others prefer the afternoon

- Make sales calls when you feel positive

- Remember, if you're working from home it can be difficult to sound businesslike when you're slouched on the sofa

YOU AS A COMMUNICATOR

THE PRACTICE
TUNE IN TO YOUR CALLER

Super-Users tune in to their caller's requirements.

- The caller who is in a hurry wants you to be brisk and efficient
- The caller who is in the mood for a chat wants you to take your time
- The caller who is distressed needs your empathy
- The caller who has a complaint wants understanding and action
- The caller who contacts a care-line or a help-desk wants guidance and advice

Aim to get on the same 'wave-length'.

YOU AS A COMMUNICATOR

THE PRACTICE
WEAR THE RIGHT HAT

From call to call and even within the same call, Super-Users instinctively know which role to take on:

The Type of Call	The Role
"I'd like to buy... Please send me..."	The Provider
"What should I do about...? How can I...?" "Which would you...?"	The Adviser
Distressed caller needing empathy, understanding and reassurance	The Supporter
Getting the caller out of a difficult situation	The Rescuer
Solving the caller's problems and complaint handling	The Problem Solver

To switch between and perform each of these roles you need to **ask questions** and **listen actively**.

THE PRACTICE

USEFUL TYPES OF QUESTIONS

Open questions are used to gain more information:

- "How long will it take me to...?"
- "What information will be needed if...?"

Open questions usually begin with the words:
Who, What, Why, When, Where or How

Closed questions produce a "yes", "no" or short, direct answer. They're useful for establishing facts. Examples:

- "Does your company have a training department?"
- "Will the goods be delivered on Monday or Tuesday?"

THE PRACTICE

USEFUL TYPES OF QUESTIONS (Cont'd)

Probing questions search for details:

- "Exactly how did this happen?"
- "What steps did you take?"

Reflective questions are formed by repeating or summarising what someone has said. They show that you understand. For example:

- "So you're really not happy with the way this has been handled?"
- "You're not comfortable with the new arrangements?"

Use them:

- When solving problems
- To help defuse emotional situations

THE PRACTICE

TYPES OF QUESTIONS TO AVOID

Avoid using:

- **Leading questions** which only confirm your viewpoint:
    - "I take it that you haven't...?"
    - "Don't you think it would be better to...?"

- **Multiple questions.** Stringing questions together both suggests and causes confusion:
    - "What, you mean they...? Well, what about...? Didn't they say anything...?"

Never ask questions for which you don't intend to get an answer.

YOU AS A COMMUNICATOR

THE PRACTICE

LISTEN ACTIVELY

Hearing is passive. Listening is active; it involves:

❶ Receiving   **❸** Interpreting   **❺** Responding

❷ Assimilating   **❹** Checking

Example:

"Have you any rooms available?" **(Receiving)**

Well we do, but that's not the real question I'm being asked. **(Assimilating)**

I expect they've got specific dates in mind and particular facilities too. I'll start by checking the dates. **(Interpreting)**

"What dates did you require, Mr. Fraser?" **(Checking)**

"We have single and double rooms on those dates. Which are you interested in?" **(Responding)**

THE PRACTICE

LISTEN ACTIVELY (Cont'd)

To help you listen actively:
- Avoid distractions
- Make sure you're comfortable
- Make notes, to give you a point of focus

To show you're listening actively:
- Use terms like "Uh huh" and "mmm"
- Don't interrupt

To check for understanding:
- Ask questions
- Summarise and repeat key points

To show that you've understood:
- Use phrases like "I see", "Of course"
- Paraphrase what's been said, "So you want me to..."

Communication can be difficult enough when you can see the other person. So when you're on the phone it's even more important to check that you understand and that you have been understood.

THE PRACTICE
SPEAKING AND SIGNALLING

When we communicate face-to-face, we use eye contact to tell others that it's their turn to speak. On the telephone we signal with a pause or a question.

When you give the signal, allow time for the other person to:

❶ Assimilate what's been said   ❸ Respond

❷ Recognise the silence signal

Once you've given the signal:

❶ Wait - be patient   ❸ Don't add a subsequent comment or question

❷ Don't override it

Be prepared for a longer silence when:

● You're negotiating   ● You've put forward a proposal or made a suggestion

● You've asked a question

YOU AS A COMMUNICATOR

THE PRACTICE
REDUCE PACE TO IMPROVE COMMUNICATION

Sometimes communication is difficult because people talk too quickly on the phone. They forget that you may need time to assimilate what you've said, or to make notes.

When you need to understand callers more clearly:
- Ask them to speak more slowly
- Paraphrase what's been said
- Take the lead in conversation; this will enable you to set the pace to suit yourself

When you need to write notes:
- Ask callers to slow down so that you can make notes; they'll usually adjust the pace to give you time
- If they're still going too fast, start repeating what they say at the speed you're writing

THE PRACTICE

USE POSITIVE LANGUAGE

Choose your words carefully.

Compare the impact these words will have:

"The department doesn't open until 9, so I won't be able to do anything until then" ...

... with these words:

"The department opens at 9, so I'll contact them first thing and get straight back to you"

And: "I don't know"
With: "I'll find out for you"

"Sorry to keep you waiting" encourages a mental response from the caller of "So you should be!".

"Thank you for holding" encourages a mental response of "That's all right".

YOU AS THE CALLER'S CONTACT

YOU CHOOSE

You can boost the business of your competitors:

- 9 out of 10 customers who experience a badly handled call would prefer to stop dealing with the offending organisation

Or you can boost your own:

- Each year, millions of people recommend companies to other prospective customers because they experience good telephone service

Umm, Efficient people

YOU AS THE CALLER'S CONTACT

10 WAYS TO GIVE CALLERS A **<u>BAD</u>** EXPERIENCE

✗   Make it difficult for them to find your number
✗   Be constantly engaged
✗   Pass them from department to department
✗   Make them repeat their story each time you transfer them
✗   Put them on hold and force them to listen to music they dislike
✗   Treat them as a 'nobody'
✗   Tell them it's not your job/fault/policy/problem
✗   Make them feel as though they're being 'processed'
✗   Don't give them a satisfactory solution
✗   Forget to do what you said you would do

KNOW WHAT YOUR CALLER WANTS

As 'junk' mail increases, as adverts become more interactive and as marketing techniques become more sophisticated, we become more aware of our rights as customers. Consequently, our expectations have risen.

We know we have choice and we become more demanding. We develop a philosophy which says that if you don't meet our needs, we'll find someone who does.

So what do they want? **All** callers want **C.A.S.H.**

C onvenience

A ction

S peed

H assle-free

CALLERS WANT C.A.S.H.

C onvenience - Minimum effort
- Available 24 hours a day, 7 days a week

A ction - Results are required (people don't often make calls out of idle curiosity; they generally need something; they expect action)

S peed - The call is answered promptly
- They get through to the right person easily
- Their call is treated with urgency
- The call results in immediate action

H assle-free - Calls are often made because there is a problem; the caller wants you to take responsibility and to deliver results in a hassle-free manner

YOU AS THE CALLER'S CONTACT

10 WAYS TO GIVE CALLERS A **GOOD** EXPERIENCE

- ✔ Treat them as an individual
- ✔ Listen to them
- ✔ Show understanding and empathy
- ✔ Make them feel they're important to you
- ✔ Deal with their call efficiently
- ✔ Accept responsibility
- ✔ Respond promptly and act immediately
- ✔ Give them the result they want
- ✔ Make a follow-up call
- ✔ Exceed their expectations

In short, treat your callers as you'd like to be treated!

YOU AS THE CALLER'S CONTACT

EXCEED THEIR EXPECTATIONS

Add value

- Go one step further; make a special effort; do something extra - "While you're on the line would you like me to..."

Under promise, over deliver

- Allow for it to get to them by the end of the week and then make sure it gets to them by Wednesday

Call them

- Check that everything went according to plan; find out if there's anything else you can do

ANSWERING THE PHONE

An unanswered phone or one that is left to ring for a long time may be:

- A lost opportunity
- A way to upset the caller

Answer a call promptly. Three or four rings of the phone will give you time to:

- Stop what you're doing
- Prepare to answer the phone
- Pick it up and announce yourself

Answer a call efficiently:

- Have a pen and paper ready to take notes
- Announce yourself clearly

ANNOUNCING YOURSELF
WHAT YOU SAY IF IT'S YOUR PHONE

Just saying "Hello" can waste time:

"Hello"
"Is that Ponds Corporation?"
"Yes"
"I want the sales department please."
"This is the sales department."

Announce yourself using a combination of:

- A greeting - "Good morning/Good afternoon"
- Your company name or department
- Your own name

Use two of the above options. Using all three is trying for the caller and for you. If you need to repeat all three regularly it becomes difficult to say with enthusiasm.

ANNOUNCING YOURSELF
WHAT YOU SAY IF IT'S SOMEONE ELSE'S PHONE

When you answer someone else's phone you will
almost certainly need to take a message, so:

- Get a pen and paper first
- Then answer the phone

Let the caller know that you're answering
on behalf of someone else:

"Megan Tudor's phone, Penny Lloyd speaking."

YOU AS THE CALLER'S CONTACT

ANNOUNCING YOURSELF

HOW YOU SAY IT

Even when the phone is answered with "Hello?" you can tell if that person is happy or sad, bored or busy, hassled or pleased to get a call.

How will **your** announcement sound?

Smiling when you announce yourself can help to make you sound pleased to receive the call.

Remember, you don't know who is on the end of the phone and first impressions count.

YOU AS THE CALLER'S CONTACT

USING ANSWERING SYSTEMS

Answering systems can be used to record messages when you're unavailable.

Help the caller by:

- Giving clear instructions
- Using an appropriate tone and style of message
- Respecting their time with a concise message
- Dealing with your messages regularly
- Getting back to them promptly

"PLEASE SPEAK AFTER THE TONE"

YOU AS THE CALLER'S CONTACT

TAKING CALLS FOR OTHERS

When you're asked to take calls for others make sure you're properly briefed. Find out:

- Where they're going (for your information only)
- If there are any circumstances in which you should contact them and how you can do this
- When they will be back
- Who they may be expecting calls from
- How they would like calls handled
- How they would like messages passed on

TAKING A MESSAGE

ESTABLISHING THE DETAILS

- Find out:
    - the name of the caller
    - their organisation
    - their contact details
    - a time when they can be contacted
    - the message
    - specific action required

- Repeat this information back to the caller

- Double-check spellings and contact details

A phone message pad can be a useful reminder of all the details you need.

48

TAKING A MESSAGE

DELIVERING THE MESSAGE

- Write the message down clearly; in addition to the details you've established, add:
  - your name
  - the date and time of the call

- Deliver the message; if you need to leave a message on someone's desk, or in a message book, check later that the message has been received

- If necessary get back to callers yourself to give them a status report; "Dr. Palmer has been delayed and won't be available until tomorrow. Would you like to speak to anyone else?"

WHEN THE CALL IS NOT FOR YOU

Don't apportion blame:

- "You've got the wrong department" means that the caller's at fault
- "You've been put through to the wrong department" means that the person they dealt with before is at fault

Neither statement is helpful. Just:

- Establish the caller's situation
- Advise who the caller needs to speak to and offer to find out if that person's available
- If possible, transfer the call

YOU AS THE CALLER'S CONTACT

TRANSFERRING A CALL - STEP 1

When you find that a call should be handled by someone else:

- Give the caller the name of the correct person and offer to find out if s/he is available
- Explain to the caller what you are about to do (put the call on hold, go to the next office, etc)
- Tell the caller what will happen next (hear nothing, a regular bleep, etc)
- Give the caller a realistic estimate of the time you will take

TRANSFERRING A CALL - STEP 2

If the person the caller needs to speak to is able to take the call:

- Pass on full details of the caller and caller's situation
- Tell the caller that you are able to transfer the call and that you've explained the situation
- Give the caller the name and extension number of the person about to take the call, in case the transfer fails
- Transfer the call

If the person the caller needs to speak to is not able to take the call, offer to take a message, or provide contact details so that the caller can try again.

GETTING CUT OFF

If you get cut off during a call, remember that:

- The person who made the call should dial again
- The person who received the call should put the receiver down and wait for the caller to phone again
- If you're dealing with a system that uses a switchboard and you're cut off when transferring a call, let the switchboard operator know; the operator will be able to deal with the call more efficiently

FIRST/LAST IMPRESSIONS ARE LASTING

First impressions

- Greet people as though you were meeting them face-to-face - smile and give a verbal handshake
- Make them feel the call will be worthwhile

Last impressions

- Sign off with the equivalent of a warm friendly handshake - use their name
- Smile as you speak
- Thank them
- Don't put the receiver down until they've said goodbye too!

KNOW WHAT IT'S LIKE TO CALL YOU

- Are you easy to contact?
- Is the line always busy?
- Does the phone ring for ages?
- Is your message-taking system effective?
- What do you sound like on the phone?
- How do you come across to others?
- When did you last attend a telephone training session?
- What annoys you most when calling others? Do you do this to people who call you?
- Ask your friends and colleagues what they like most and hate most about dealing with you on the phone.

YOU AS THE CALLER'S CONTACT

FINDING YOUR NUMBER

Most people use Yellow Pages, the Phone Directory and Directory Enquiries to find numbers.

- How easy are you to find in the phone directory?
- Are there ways to find your number easily?
- Is it clearly placed on your publicity material?
- Do people sometimes mistake it for the fax number?
- Is it displayed so that local, national and international callers know how to use it?

You won't be able to answer these questions, but your callers will.
Listen to their answers.
Try implementing their suggestions.

TURN COMPLAINTS INTO LOYAL CUSTOMERS

Our society is becoming more confident about complaining. We no longer quietly accept the fly in the soup or the train being late. We do something about it. We complain.

If the customer complains, you've got a chance to put it right. And the satisfied complainant is more likely to return than the non-complainant.

If they don't complain, they simply vote with their feet.

YOU AS THE CALLER'S CONTACT

RECEIVING A COMPLAINT
WHAT NOT TO SAY OR DO

Don't say:
- ✗ "I don't see what the problem is."
- ✗ "Could you call back tomorrow?"
- ✗ "It's not our policy."
- ✗ "There's no one here who can help you."
- ✗ "You're not the first person to complain about that."

- ✗ "I'm going on holiday tomorrow."
- ✗ "I'm new here."
- ✗ "It's not my job."

And **don't**:
- ✗ Justify the problem - callers are not interested in your problems, just what you're going to do about their problem
- ✗ Make excuses - acknowledge the problem, then get on and solve it
- ✗ Make unrealistic promises
- ✗ Take it personally or allocate blame - it will result in emotional behaviour, defensiveness and aggression

RECEIVING A COMPLAINT

THE BUILDING BLOCKS FOR SUCCESS (4 As)

Attitude

- A complaint is an opportunity to improve; a positive attitude will help you handle it successfully.

Acknowledgement

- How would you feel if this happened to you? Listen actively, ask open questions, check your understanding, acknowledge there is cause for complaint, show empathy.

Agreement

- Discuss possible solutions; offer choice, reach an agreed solution which is satisfactory from the caller's viewpoint.

Action

- Keep the customer informed at all times; implement what you've agreed, call the customer to check that the solution has been satisfactory.

MANAGING AGGRESSION AND RUDENESS

Aggression

- Don't enter into an argument
- Allow the caller to let off steam
- Don't interrupt
- Put the 4 As into action

Rudeness

- Ignore the rudeness
- Don't retaliate
- Don't take it personally
- Put the 4 As into action

The 4 As (see page 59):

Attitude; **A**cknowledgement;
Agreement; **A**ction.

RECEIVING AN ENQUIRY

Don't just answer the callers' questions and let them ring off.

Make the most of their calls and find out:

- Their name
- Their contact details
- Where they heard about you
- How else you might be able to help

INTERNAL CUSTOMERS

Some telephone systems have a different ring so that you can tell if it's an internal or external call. But remember that internal callers are your customers too. They should be treated in the same way as external callers.

When you receive an internal call you should:

- Answer the phone promptly
- Announce yourself clearly
- Have a pen and paper ready
- Give callers C.A.S.H. (see page 39)

YOU AS THE CALLER

THE FACTS

Three out of every four calls to businesses do not achieve their objective on the first attempt.

Are you one of these callers?

YOU AS THE CALLER

PROBLEMS YOU MAY HAVE

Do you:

- Ever have to make a second call because you didn't ask about ...?
- Find it difficult to get through to the right person?
- Leave messages for people to call back - and they don't?
- Ever get ignored on hold or felt lost in a queuing system?
- Always get the information you need, or the outcome you want?
- Need to 'chase' people on the phone?

The answer to many of these problems is to be prepared and to follow structured techniques.

YOU AS THE CALLER

MAKING THE CALL

1. **Preparing.** Before you pick up the phone take a moment to check that the telephone is the best communications vehicle for your task. If it is, make sure you know:

- What you want to achieve
- How to get through to the person you need to speak to
- What you'll do if the person is not in
- What message you'll leave if you're greeted by an answering system
- Your opening words
- How you'll introduce yourself
- How the conversation might go: facts you must establish or give; objections that might be raised; how you might overcome those objections; etc

And have:

- All the information you might need to hand
- Facilities to take notes

MAKING THE CALL

2. **During** the call make sure you:
- Build rapport
- Listen actively
- Give feedback
- Ask questions
- Check for understanding

- Make notes
- Use your preparation notes
- Don't get distracted
- Keep focused on your aims

3. At the **end** of the call:
- Summarise the main points
- Confirm the outcome

- Agree actions

4. **After** the call:
- Check your notes for things to do
- Expand and clarify notes if they're to be kept for reference
- Take action as necessary

SPEAKING TO ANSWER MACHINES

- Listen to the instructions carefully
- Only start speaking after a given signal
- Speak clearly
- Speak slowly
- Spell names
- Repeat numbers
- Leave your name, number and a short message
- Be aware that some machines allow only a limited time for your message

YOU AS THE CALLER

GETTING THROUGH TO PEOPLE

When you know the person's name:

What you say:	What it sounds like:
1 "Adrian Lloyd please."	You're on first name terms and you're expecting to be put through
2 "Mr. Lloyd please."	Your relationship is more distanced and your request may be questioned
3 "Please may I speak to Mr. Lloyd?"	You're unsure of your rights and your request may be questioned

When you don't know the person's name make two calls:

- The first to establish the name
- The second (some time later) to use option 1

If you use this technique, don't get upset if others do it to you!

IF THEY'RE NOT AVAILABLE

Keep the ball in your court:

- Find out when they will be available
- Arrange to call again

Leaving a message for **them** to call **you** means that you:

- Lose control
- Give up the right to call them
- Risk offending them if you call before they do

HANGING ON THE LINE

Only hang on the line when either:

- Your contact knows you're there and will be with you in a few moments, or

- You've got nothing better to do and you don't mind wasting time and money

If you do get stuck in the holding system, just hang up.

71

YOU AS THE CALLER

OBTAINING INFORMATION

Prepare for the call:

- Decide what you want
- List the questions you need to ask
- Make a flow chart for the call - if the answer is "yes" to this, then ...; if the answer is "no" to that, then ...

Make the call:

- Establish the right person to speak to
- Follow your flow chart
- Check for understanding by summarising and paraphrasing
- Make sure you've covered all your points before you end the call

GETTING WHAT YOU WANT

Make sure you're dealing with the right person then, sticking to the facts and without emotion:

- State what you want (payment of an invoice)
- Find out what has to happen for you to get what you want (the manager needs to sign the cheque and she's away until Friday)
- Convert this into specifics about who will take what actions and when they will be taken ("So when the manager returns, you'll ask her to sign the cheque and I'll get it first thing on Monday morning?")
- State what follow up action you will take to make sure this happens ("You're probably busy so I'll ring on Friday just to remind you")
- Keep a progress record and, where necessary, follow up calls in writing
- Stick to your plan - persistence pays (ring first thing on Friday and find out what time the cheque will be signed; then call again at the time it should be signed - and if you feel it necessary, call once more just to check that it will make the post that day)
- Make a call to acknowledge receipt and to say thank you

YOU AS THE CALLER

MAKING A COMPLAINT

Prepare for the call:

- Write down the facts
- Write down the solution you want

Make the call:

- Speak calmly and be assertive (see page 96)
- Don't get personal - refer to the department/organisation/system, etc
- Stick to the facts
- State your desired solution
- Agree a solution - if necessary, follow it up in writing and chase it to a satisfactory solution (see previous page)

NEGOTIATING

Most negotiating situations are best dealt with face-to-face where you can see and use body language.

However, if you have a strong case to present and you're concerned about being swayed by the emotions of the other party, you may find it easier to negotiate on the phone. It will help to increase the objectivity of your communication, and keep the emotional content to a minimum.

But, remember that the result of effective negotiation is a situation where both parties are happy with the outcome.
It should be a win/win situation.

MAKING AN INTERNATIONAL CALL

- Most countries can be dialled directly
- The ringing, engaged and unobtainable tones may be different from those used in the UK; use the phone directory to find out more about these tones
- Speak clearly and pay particular attention to enunciation
- Be prepared for a slightly longer pause between you finishing a sentence and the other person starting to speak
- Be aware of the time difference between the country you're in and the country you're calling
- Know the cost - the times for 'cheap' and 'standard' charges vary from country to country

YOU AS A RAPPORT BUILDER

THE COST

It costs eight times more to recruit a new customer than to retain an old one. Telephone Super-Users help maintain customer loyalty.

10 EASY WAYS TO ALIENATE

When you receive a call:

- ✗ Be apathetic
- ✗ If they don't ask, don't tell them
- ✗ Address them incorrectly
- ✗ Tut and sigh to show that you think they're ignorant
- ✗ Lie to them

When you make a call:

- ✗ Be aggressive
- ✗ Show no respect
- ✗ Be impatient
- ✗ Be demanding
- ✗ Be rude

YOU AS A RAPPORT BUILDER

RAPPORT = RESULTS

People:

- Buy from people they like
- Will recommend people they like
- Do things for people they like
- Will go one step further for people they like

Whether you're making or receiving a call your relationship with the other person will affect the outcome.

Building rapport establishes a relationship which says:

- You are important to me
- I value you
- I will treat you as an individual

YOU AS A RAPPORT BUILDER

USING RAPPORT

Use rapport to:

- ✔ Increase customer loyalty
- ✔ Build long-term relationships
- ✔ Show you care
- ✔ Help relax a nervous or flustered caller
- ✔ Defuse an angry caller
- ✔ Ease a difficult conversation
- ✔ Calm an emotional caller
- ✔ Make the caller feel special
- ✔ Generate a positive image
- ✔ Get results

YOU AS A RAPPORT BUILDER

WAYS TO BUILD RAPPORT

Build rapport on the phone by:

- Answering the phone promptly
- Giving a genuine greeting
- Reinforcing your words with gestures (eg: smiling)
- Using the caller's name
- Treating the caller as an individual
- Showing an understanding of the caller's situation
- Giving the caller undivided attention
- Thanking the caller - for time/call/understanding/actions/and so on
- Being proactive; call back, seek feedback

To build rapport with someone you know you can also:

- Add a statement of recognition to your greeting
- Ask about the caller's circumstances

YOU AS A RAPPORT BUILDER

SAYING "THANK YOU"

Saying "thank you" is a simple way to build rapport and leave a positive image. Find a way to say "thank you" for each call. Some may be harder than others, but they all need to be genuine.

- Thank you for your time/help/call/suggestions
- Or, maybe, for more difficult calls, Thank you for listening/understanding/patience/honesty

Try to extend and reinforce the "thank you" when the call is over. Put your thanks in writing - send a letter or card.

YOU AS A RAPPORT BUILDER

CONSISTENCY

Rapport requires consistency. Being consistent:

- Reinforces the image you project
- Confirms the perceptions and expectations of others

In a company, consistency can be helped by:

- Encouraging everyone to use a similar style of greeting
- Encouraging a positive phone culture
- Having a policy for using the telephone
- Monitoring each other's performance
- Providing continuous telephone training for staff at all levels

YOU AS A SUPER-USER

WHAT MAKES THE DIFFERENCE?

The Super-User's Oath

"I will be in charge and make the phone work for me."

"I will seek out time-eaters and destroy them."

"I will use Super-User control techniques at all times."

YOU AS A SUPER-USER

THE SUPER-USER'S OATH

"I WILL BE IN CHARGE AND MAKE THE PHONE WORK FOR ME"

1. Get organised

Organise your phone environment:

- Make the phone accessible
- Keep the area around the phone clear
- Position the phone to give as much privacy as possible
- Place it in a quiet area, away from noise
- Keep a notepad and pen beside the phone

Position your phone so you can be comfortable:

- Make the phone easy to reach
- Discomfort will distract you
- Your posture will affect your voice

YOU AS A SUPER-USER

THE SUPER-USER'S OATH

"I WILL BE IN CHARGE AND MAKE THE PHONE WORK FOR ME"

2. Use all the features

Use all the features your phone provides. Just using pre-programmed numbers and last number redial facilities can easily save an hour in a busy week. Features include:

- Last number redial
- Memory store for frequently used numbers
- Automatic dialling
- Mute/secrecy button
- Transfer and recall
- Remote pickup
- On-hook dialling
- Hands-free speech
- Ringer volume control
- Speaker volume switch
- Taping or electronically recording the conversation

THE SUPER-USER'S OATH

"I WILL BE IN CHARGE AND MAKE THE PHONE WORK FOR ME"

3. Use the technology

The telecommunications industry moves quickly. Keep up-to-date with new services and products.

Useful phone services include:

● Call return	● Reminder call	● Caller display
● Call diversion	● 3-way calling	● Ring-back
● Call waiting	● Charge advice	● Call sign

Use products such as mobile phones, answering systems that can be accessed remotely, and services such as e-mail and text messaging to help you make the most of your time.

THE SUPER-USER'S OATH

"I WILL BE IN CHARGE AND MAKE THE PHONE WORK FOR ME"

4. Use a mobile phone with care

No, this is not a health warning - although you should be aware that increasing attention is being paid to research in this area. This is a warning about the mobile phone and your image.

Mobiles are great when used in the right circumstances. However, by their very nature, they encourage us to break every Super-User rule in the book:

- You answer them and make calls from them while you're on the move and when you're doing other things
- Pen and paper are rarely to hand
- You allow them to interrupt you
- You answer by saying "Hello?"
- Background noise and weak signals can make communication difficult and sometimes even tiresome for the person you're calling
- It can be difficult to answer promptly - first you have to realise it's your briefcase that's ringing, and by the time you've dealt with the security lock on the case, the caller has rung off!

THE SUPER-USER'S OATH

"I WILL BE IN CHARGE AND MAKE THE PHONE WORK FOR ME"

4. Use a mobile phone with care (cont'd)

For all its amazing, 'wouldn't-be-without-it' attributes, a mobile phone can seriously damage your image if you don't treat it with respect.

A few simple guidelines:

- Be considerate to others around you
- Don't shout into the mouthpiece
- A poor connection or a low battery does nothing for your image
- When you're going into a meeting switch the phone off or leave it outside with a colleague
- Observe and respect mobile-free zones
- Be aware of the cost
- Consider texting or e-mailing rather than talking
- Don't let your mobile rule your life - plan some time without it

THE SUPER-USER'S OATH

"I WILL SEEK OUT TIME-EATERS..."

Be aware of how you spend your time on the phone. Keep a diary for at least a week to make a record of:

- The number of incoming and outgoing calls
- Who you call and who calls you
- The time you spend on the phone
- When you make calls and when others call you
- The type of calls you make and receive
- The purpose of the calls
- The result of the call - conclusive or further action

Use this information to identify what eats your time.

THE SUPER-USER'S OATH

"...AND DESTROY THEM"

Too much time spent on the phone:

- Prepare for the call
- Decide how much time it should take
- Tell the other person that you have limited time for the call
- Keep a watch, clock (or egg timer!) in view
- If you don't need immediate feedback, consider calling when the person is out so that you just leave a message. Or send them an e-mail or text message
- If you do need feedback, call just before you know the person's going out - allow just enough time, but not too much; use this technique sparingly
- Gain and maintain control

Frequently interrupted by calls:

- Create dedicated times for using and not using the phone
- Tell regular callers when to call
- Use an answering system or ask a colleague to take your calls for an appropriate length of time

THE SUPER-USER'S OATH

"... AND DESTROY THEM" (Cont'd)

Troubled by time wasters:

- Take the lead to keep ramblers and chatterers to the point
- Redirect callers you should not really be speaking to
- Terminate the call:
    - be polite, thank them for their call
    - be firm, tell them that you're not interested
    - be gone, say goodbye and replace the receiver

Making lame excuses or using delaying tactics only:

- Gives callers the right to call again
- Makes it harder for you to say "no" and mean it

YOU AS A SUPER-USER

THE SUPER-USER'S OATH

"I WILL USE SUPER-USER CONTROL TECHNIQUES"

1. Plan

Thinking before you get on the phone saves time, money and face, so use a call sheet.
Using call sheets:

- ✔ Saves time
- ✔ Increases chances of achieving aim
- ✔ Provides a record of the call
- ✔ Reminds you of actions to be taken
- ✔ Improves call technique

Design your own call sheet and include headings such as:

- Name; company; date; time
- Purpose; content; structure
- Response; objections
- Outcomes; actions

Or use a software programme especially designed for your computer.

THE SUPER-USER'S OATH

"I WILL USE SUPER-USER CONTROL TECHNIQUES"

2. Be equal

Calling people 'sir' or 'madam' while they use your first name makes them more dominant and gives them more control. Getting on first name terms is a way to give you equal status on the phone.

However, social etiquette, cultural differences or company policy may mean that it's not appropriate for you to be on first-name terms with your caller. In these circumstances use other mechanisms, such as asking questions, to take control.

When you need to be more **assertive** on the phone try:

- **Standing up** - your voice will sound stronger; you will feel more in control
- **Using body language** - gestures and movements emphasise your words and bring meaning to them; use them on the phone too
- **Repeating caller's name** during the conversation to reinforce equal status
- **Giving yourself time to think** by reflecting back what's just been said; alternatively, establish the facts, arrange to get back to the caller, and get off the phone

THE SUPER-USER'S OATH

"I WILL USE SUPER-USER CONTROL TECHNIQUES"

3. Reduce stress

- Use a phone with a pleasant ring - some tones jar or grate
- Adjust the volume of the ringer to make it softer and less intrusive
- When the phone rings, finish speaking/writing your sentence before you pick it up
- Don't put off difficult or important calls
- Organise your environment - aim for comfort; reduce clutter and distractions
- Be prepared to receive calls - always keep a pen and paper to hand
- Be prepared when making calls - organise yourself before you dial
- When you re-charge your mobile consider what you might do to 're-charge' yourself
- Take a break after a stressful call
- Plan times away from the phone

THE SUPER-USER'S OATH

"I WILL USE SUPER-USER CONTROL TECHNIQUES"

4. Control interruptions

When you're on the phone reduce interruptions by:
- Making your calls where you will not be distracted
- Telling others that you will be unavailable
- Arranging for someone to cover for you
- Shutting your door, if you have one
- Displaying a 'do not disturb' sign

If you do get interrupted when you're on the phone:
- Wait for a convenient break in the conversation
- Excuse yourself to the caller
- Use the mute/secrecy button so the caller doesn't hear you
- Write down a word/phrase that will enable you to pick up your conversation again quickly
- Make arrangements to deal with the interruption - don't deal with it there and then, it will only encourage people to continue interrupting you
- Thank your caller for waiting (don't apologise) and resume your conversation

THE SUPER-USER'S OATH

"I WILL USE SUPER-USER CONTROL TECHNIQUES"

4. Control interruptions (cont'd)

If you're in a meeting or don't wish to be disturbed, reduce interruptions from phone calls by:

- Asking someone else to take your calls
- Arranging to re-route your calls to someone else's phone
- Using an answering system to take calls for you
- Turning your mobile off

If you do get interrupted by a phone call:

- Tell the caller that it's not convenient to take the call now
- Arrange a suitable time to return the call

THE SUPER-USER'S OATH

"I WILL USE SUPER-USER CONTROL TECHNIQUES"

5. Delegate

Brief well, make sure you tell them:
- Where you're going, when you'll be back and how to contact you
- In what circumstances you can be contacted/interrupted
- Who you are expecting calls from
- How you would like calls handled and messages dealt with

Empower the person:
- Give enough information to enable the person to be more than just a message taking service

Encourage responsibility:
- Encourage the person to deal with the calls where possible - it will be more satisfactory for the caller and will save you time

Reciprocate the arrangement:
- One good turn deserves another

THE SUPER-USER'S OATH

"I WILL USE SUPER-USER CONTROL TECHNIQUES"

6. Take the lead

On outgoing calls:

- Be prepared
- Structure your call

On incoming calls:

- **L**isten to the caller
- **E**stablish the purpose of the call
- **A**ssess the situation
- **D**irect the conversation

THE SUPER-USER'S OATH

"I WILL USE SUPER-USER CONTROL TECHNIQUES"

7. Ask questions

The person asking the questions is the one in control of the conversation. Use questions to structure and control your conversation. It may be like this:

Type of question	When receiving a call	When making a call
Closed	To establish or confirm information	Establishing you're talking to the right person or that it's a convenient time to call
Open	Establishing the nature of the call	Getting the conversation going
Probing	Gathering specific details of requirements	Narrowing the conversation to specifics
Reflective	Checking for and showing understanding	
Closed	Finishing the conversation	

For information on the different types of questions and other ways to use them see pages 27-29.

THE SUPER-USER'S OATH

"I WILL USE SUPER-USER CONTROL TECHNIQUES"

7. Ask questions (cont'd)

The way you phrase your questions is important. Choose your words carefully. Strong questions make you sound in control and help you to achieve your aims.

Making an appointment:

Weak:

"Would it be possible for me to visit you some time next week?"

Strong:

"It sounds as though we should meet. Which day is more convenient for you, Tuesday or Wednesday?"

THE SUPER-USER'S OATH

"I WILL USE SUPER-USER CONTROL TECHNIQUES"

8. Use precision endings

When you need to end a call:

Signal Indicate that the call is coming to an end
Summarise Briefly recap agreements, decisions, etc
Sign-off Say "goodbye" and be gone

A signal must be given in time for:

- The receiver to respond accordingly
- A summary
- A sign-off

Short calls: signal at the beginning of the call

Longer calls: signal when you have a few minutes left

THE SUPER-USER'S OATH

"I WILL USE SUPER-USER CONTROL TECHNIQUES"

8. Use precision endings (cont'd)

Once you've given a signal, stick to it. A false signal is like crying wolf - your callers will learn to ignore them.

Either excuse yourself or excuse them.

Excusing yourself ("I've only got a few minutes...") puts the onus on you. Be aware that your tone of voice and choice of words can either indicate that the call is important or that you have better and more important things to do.

Excusing them ("I know you're busy so...") may appeal to their ego but in the wrong tone of voice may sound patronising.

THE SUPER-USER'S OATH

"I WILL USE SUPER-USER CONTROL TECHNIQUES"

9. Call them before they call you

You lose control when you:

- Put off a difficult call
- Wait for someone to call you back
- Are 'too busy' to phone

Calling them before they call you means that you can:

- ✔ Prepare for the call
- ✔ Be in control
- ✔ Maximise your chances of achieving your aims

THE SUPER-USER'S OATH

"I WILL USE SUPER-USER CONTROL TECHNIQUES"

10. Say when it's not convenient

Think twice about taking calls if:

- You haven't got the necessary information to hand
- You're about to leave
- You're in the middle of something else
- You're in your car
- You're likely to irritate someone else

Don't compromise your communication.
If it's not convenient to take the call, say so, and arrange to call back.

THE CHOICE IS YOURS

So, there are 3 easy steps to taking the 'oath' and becoming a Super-User. Will you take them? Can you afford not to?

On page 14 you probably realised that the answer to the big question was "No".

So, use the techniques described in this Pocketbook, develop Super-User skills and win:

- ✔ Customers
- ✔ Orders
- ✔ Opportunities
- ✔ Business
- ✔ Credibility
- ✔ Promotion
- ✔ Jobs

In today's world, you can't afford not to be a **SUPER-USER**!

About the Author

Mary Richards has a background in education, international marketing and general management. Many years of designing and delivering training to public and private sector organisations, the old and the young, the willing and the resistant have provided Mary with a wealth of experience which she now uses to create business skills publications and resource materials for trainers. In parallel, Mary actively explores the links between the mind, the emotions, and the body's structure and energy systems. She is the author of *'The Stress Pocketbook'* in this series.

Published by Management Pocketbooks Ltd
Laurel House, Station Approach, Alresford, Hants SO24 9JH, U.K.

© Mary Richards

First edition 1997 ISBN 1 870471 46 6
This edition published 2007 ISBN 978 1 903776 84 1

British Library Cataloguing-in-Publication Data – A catalogue record for this book
is available from the British Library.

Design typesetting and graphics by **Efex ltd** Printed in UK.

ORDER FORM

Your details

Name _____

Position _____

Company _____

Address _____

_____

_____

Telephone _____

Fax _____

E-mail _____

VAT No. (EC companies) _____

Your Order Ref _____

Please send me:

		No. copies
The Telephone Skills	Pocketbook	☐
The _____	Pocketbook	☐
The _____	Pocketbook	☐
The _____	Pocketbook	☐

Order by Post
MANAGEMENT POCKETBOOKS LTD
LAUREL HOUSE, STATION APPROACH,
ALRESFORD, HAMPSHIRE SO24 9JH UK
Order by Phone, Fax or Internet
Telephone: +44 (0)1962 735573
Facsimile: +44 (0)1962 733637
E-mail: sales@pocketbook.co.uk
Web: www.pocketbook.co.uk

Customers in USA should contact:
Management Pocketbooks
2427 Bond Street, University Park, IL 60466
Telephone: 866 620 9944   Facsimile: 708 534 7803
E-mail: mp.orders@ware-pak.com
Web: www.managementpocketbooks.com